Gracious Nature

Poems on Earth and Life

by

Robert J. Tiess

PRINT EDITION ISBN-13:
979-8-9861795-7-5

Cover photograph by: Robert J. Tiess

Printed in the United States of America

Dedication

For Sandra,
my wife,

and in memory
of my parents.

Welcome!

Welcome, dear friend, to my third poetry collection!

I love nature, and I enjoy exploring the natural world through poetry. The poems in this book are part of my continuous journey, as a poet and a person, to contemplate and appreciate Earth, nature, and all forms of life.

Nature generously enriches existence with essential light, precious water, invigorating wind, diverse plants and animals, teeming landscapes, copious cycles of growth and renewal, abundant and ubiquitous beauty, and many natural wonders and resources.

Without asking, we receive a wealth of considerations and potential lessons every day from our planet. There's so much to witness, so much to treasure, and we have countless connections to discover between the small, the personal, the global, and the universal.

I'm grateful to share my love of nature with you, and I hope my poems inspire you to reflect more upon natural happenings and to rejoice in the magnificence of existence.

Wishing you profuse peace,
limitless inspiration,
and continuous joy,

Robert

Table of Contents

The Poems: Part One 10

Nature Preserves 11

Gracious Nature 12

Birdcalls 15

The Music of the Wolves 16

Mud Lessons 18

Cetacean... 19

To a Dandelion 20

Salve 22

Peak Humility..23

Set...24

Unhurried...26

Spare 27

Natural Geometries......................................29

Palliative.. 31

Snowpack 32

Overcoming 33

Sea Turtle Circles..34

Utopia for Deer 37

Finding Yourself in the Universal Mirror 38

Part Two.. 40

Enlightening 41

Dawn after Storms.....................................42

Date Palm (Phoenix Dactylifera) 43

For Real 44

Oak Noticing 45

Cloudscape 46

Libretto 47

Curatorial Tutorial......................................48

Nuptials 49

Rubato 51

Carrion 53

Recipe for Mass Extinction Number Six 54

To a Crocus..55

Arboreal Time 56

Breaching 58

Coming to Light 59

Nature Retreat 60

Away 61

Elsewhere in the Universe 62

Plainspoken...63

Revival 64

On High Point, New Jersey 65

Part Three 67

Bedrock Awakening 68

Peaceable Earth Beginning with Me... 70

Outreach 71

Rewilding 73

Human Natural..74

The Rapids vs. River Birch 76

Said a Tree at Sycamore Canyon....................77

Befriending Nature 78

Great Egrets 79

An Hour in the Life of a Snowshoe Hare 80

Consulting the Oak 81

Vernal Equinox 83

Entwining Light 84

While Shoveling 85

To the Full Moon.................................... 86

Floriculture 87

Rendering 88

Stems..89

Crystalline 90

Notices 91

Audience...92

Part Four 93

Kindred of the Earth 94

At One's Disposal..................................95

Weather Proof...96

Canadian Wildfire Smoke in New York City......98

Arches National Park....................................99

Before a Minimalist Landscape....................100

Sakura Selflessness....................................101

A Prayer for the Squirrel............................102

Diamond Reflections.................................103

Travel Magic..104

On the Nature and History of Influence........105

The Rocks Remembering............................106

To the Woods of Livelihood........................107

Forty Minutes on the Mountain...................108

Said...109

Inaudible..110

If We Are Stardust....................................111

Quenched...112

Openness..113

To a Blue Spruce......................................114

Part Five..115

Fisheye Lens..116

Interstitial..117

Save..118

Muted..119

Touching Textures....................................120

The Careful Hare......................................121

Crop Rotations...123

Moonflowering 124

Earth for a Day 126

Luna Moth 129

To the Stars 130

Squirrel for an Afternoon 131

Imperative 132

Unbeknownst 133

Considering the Cows 134

Part Six 135

Planting Marigolds 136

Continuous 137

To the Manatees 138

Scales 139

Progress 141

Craft 142

Against Noise Pollution 143

Towards a More Natural Meditation 144

Sandstone 148

Effortless 150

Rain Gauging 151

Autumn in Reverse 152

Part Seven 153

Soil of Life 154

Original Liberty 156

Lineage 157

Neighborly 158

More Intimate Cosmology 159

Running with the Seagulls 160

To the Sky 161

Entwined 169

The Daring of the Roadside Deer 170

Repose 172

Earthward 173

Versed in Earth 175

Fields of Study 177

Reckoning 179

Little Gratitudes 180

Going Speechless 181

Before, Ahead 184

Afterwords 188

Essay: On the Vitality of Nature Poems 189

About the Author 196

Other Books by the Author 197

The Poems: Part One

Nature Preserves

It's dawn: please let me pause to thank the earth
for all this beauty, music, fragrance, light.

See, once I had no time or mind for them—

    red robins bobbing in the garden bath,
    the woodchucks munching on the hickory bark,
    goldfinches straining over sparrow songs,
    those tightrope squirrels walking power lines,
    or morning glories baring all their souls.

That was when life meant waking, working, sleep
—obligatory cycles of demands,
constraints of contracts, cubicles, long calls
between fluorescent fixtures, frosted glass,
and dismal windows thick with city bricks.

Then my car died. I trekked up grassy hills,
by woods I'd driven past, down streets for blocks.
Sometimes I spotted deer, raccoons, a skunk,
or wind blew music through the changing leaves,
or sunlit spiderwebs would catch my eyes.

In those essential months I grew to find
how nature saved me from my daily grind.

Gracious Nature

Now nature's *gracious*,
as in *kind*

—so kind that life seems viable,
abundant,
near magnanimous,

sustained by altruistic earth,
which generously lends much wealth:

    this soil that lets harvests grow
    and suffers every burial,

    this water cleansing, ending thirst,
    renewing and replenishing,

    —then air the living love to breathe,

    and light divulging miracles,
    this paradise of snakes and all.

And *gracious* stands for *merciful*,
such leniency that lets us stray,
refashion fields,
seize reserves,

invade,
pollute,
consume good fruit,

yet be forgiven for these sins
because Earth yet indulges us,
affords us comforts,
luxuries

—such ease we often figure must exist,
no matter how we might defile the sky
or sabotage essential habitats
or postulate extinction cannot be.

We should concede *we know*
(and always knew,
if we are being truthful with ourselves)

this charity's exhaustible.

What tolerance or hospitality
we've counted on
across our lavish years
was momentary,
finite from the start.

Yes, even Eden had an edge

      —a gate—
      —a passage
      to be crossed once,
      only once—

deciding where benevolence
trailed off
and vegetation turned
to burning dust,

     where agony would slither,
     rattle onward,

          hissing,
          soon constricting,
          ruthless in its chase,

then sinking
venomous fangs
into the dream of grace.

Birdcalls

I love to eavesdrop on the birds,
primarily in springtime, when
they come back home from far away,
excitedly discussing trips,
discovered sights, adventures, love,
above the caws and courtship songs,
the whistles in the waking woods.

These urgent chirps, recurring tweets,
and pressing peeps divulge so much,
as I sit listening on my porch,
conjecturing discussions held:

landmarks recalled, directions asked,
long entertaining anecdotes

—the conversations of our lives.

The Music of the Wolves

The operas of the wolves howl on,
not near us, here,

no, not too near,

though close enough we'd plainly hear
(if we could listen outside fear)
those overlapping arias
converging toward a choral wail
between the tundra and the cliffs,
where longing lyrics fall at once
and bow before the ocean's song
that swallows every wallowing.

These plaintive strains,
they soothe and haunt,
depending on our points of view:

if this is sadness,
what they sing,
and if despair is natural,

or if you care to wonder why
some distant being starts to cry,
now moonlight soothes the austere scene
and other creatures seem to sing.

We say we comprehend the wolves:
they bay to warn or call their packs,
seek out new mates, or mark their land

—as if that's all we'd understand,
these primal instincts we'll ascribe

—though deer and elk innately know
to move where wolfish music's faint

—where sanctuary's silence, calm,
apart from dramas, hungers, prey,

—until the vultures curve their way

—or death conspires with the night
while nocturnes veil a fight or flight.

Mud Lessons

The mud's one tough instructor here
on slopes the rain made difficult
to memorize or navigate.
Just getting home's my homework now.

Each step's a lesson with a test
I pass or fail and fall at once,
and there's much study to be made
of gaining footholds in the earth.

The mud professes patience, care
of shifting weight and placing feet,
deliberate progress, reading grounds,
This is my course in every sense.

The rugged land I'd go around
on drier days in early spring,
I welcome that, the rocks, and what
contributes to stability.

I scale a hill with sodden boots
yet little time to kick them clean:
the rain returns, and mud's not done.
My graduation's gradual.

Cetacean

The blue whales quake their salty depths
with oceanic lyrics borne
by melodies which swim outside
the beaches of our noticing.

Unhurried, ringing leagues away,
their steady serenading hums
beyond shushing of the waves,
blue pressures of dense emptiness,

whole slow notes, low tones billowing
with rhythmic will against the chills,
past tempos thrashed out by the tides.
There's learning in this listening:

I feared my drowning—death of sound,
—that sinking sense no one could care
to hear my songs or search my words
—that all these verses were for naught.

Then whales would teach me how to plunge
and cast my vocals through the hush,
ignored or not—alive for song
—for something deeper than the sea!

Though inattentive fish drift by
while sharks enforce obscurity,
now I'm my own whale, surfacing.
My song's my life, and I will sing!

To a Dandelion

Between the clover
and the vines
that climb and cling
to rotting wood,
how quietly
you preach release
from every corner
of the yard.

You bloom
a hundred rays or more
of gold that mostly
no one wants,
but you press on
with precious roots,
enduring though
ephemeral.

No withering
will limit you;
it's in this "death,"
this letting go,
that you divulge
renewal's truths
as seeds emerge,
drift off with wind:

accept this life
is brevity,
yet yielding brings
continuance,
advances past
apparent loss.
You're not there,
then you're everywhere.

Salve

Wide swaths of switchgrass lean, return,
while fingertips of wind glide forth
and gently wend through golden strands.

Each easy, long, unhurried pass
bestows a breezy tenderness
that tempers and relieves the scene.

Rainwater salves old crackled earth
now furrowed as a newfound marsh
recovering from bouts of drought.

White sky, spread like a comforter,
helps cushion sunlight's welcome warmth
upon the convalescing range.

Across this prairie countenance
of stricken heartland underneath,
an overdue peace comes at last:

a healing feeling rallies life
to hold its ground, establish roots,
emerge with purpose, resurrect

—a sense that stems from history,
if you had known the languishing
then recognized the flourishing.

Peak Humility

At
the
mountaintop,
humility's foundational:
I mustn't confuse ascent
with mastery, or equate the peak
with me, or compare that panorama
with my incapacity to hold and know the range.

Set

As four more seasons wheel by,
  December's questions shadow me
  through February into March,
  when grass gains ground and snow retreats,
  revealing what was mostly there,
  in patches I have passed with eyes
  too keen or green to recognize
  the beauty of inconstancy.

Old lands will vary. Days raise change:
  once muddy stretches settle, dry
  in regions you might walk without
  the sudden risk of stumbling
  or being swallowed up in earth.
  That barren field no one's tilled
  lends nectar, shelter, butterflies.
  New spruce revive the mountainside.

Before what seems to outlive us,
  no answers sprung from months or stars.
  Potentials swelled in sinless darkness,
  worlds of flaming yet to spark,
  creation waiting, time's designs
  of purposed futures burgeoning
  inside a mind beyond our thoughts,
  where deathless dreams weave wakeful light.

In winter there's a quilt I'll draw
  when chilled or fearful of the void
  —that fabric of the universe
  so thick, despite its emptiness,
  with patterns stitched, so intricate
  it's tempting to conceive machines
  or random grandeur fashioned this
  —but love and summer set me right!

Unhurried

As long it takes to rake these leaves
left over from this morning's storm,
my snail friend "Cheetah" crossed the stretch
between the garden and the drive,
around three meters, give or take,
while I'm still near my starting point.

He's quick in his way, fast enough,
considering he's got one foot
and hauls his home just everywhere
—that shell he shoulders all his life.
His tempo never holds him back,
unlike my haste and eagerness:

for all my rushing, I'm not near
the place I thought I ought to be,
but he's still moving, inch by inch,
unhurried by impatience, stress,
the human need to speed, not wait.
Now Cheetah's by the busted gate

—he's mocking my velocity

or modeling tenacity.

Spare

These stairs and pathways we've devised
—they spoil us with level ground,
tried passages through strange terrain,
concrete where mud would cover us
once we slogged through the bog and brush
with instinct, purpose, little more
than hunger, primal urgency.

No longer do we walk, aware
of what was written in these leaves,
the verse of earth, this cursive wind,
these passages in crackled stone.
Today, we ask our satellites,
the networks, A.I., GPS,
and still we wonder how we're lost.

Here, any woods could swallow us.
Old rivers fill us with distrust.
The mountains pound us with their shocks
of ruggedness and crushing heights.
We break from rainfall: we might melt.
We fly from lightning, now we're struck
by wilderness, the feral risk.

I've wandered never far enough,
not further than the standard fears
of rabies, snakes, the jagged rocks,

which snap at me like lions' teeth
—and I'm like Daniel in this den,
the tame one praying angels come
to spare me from such savagery.

Natural Geometries

How things in nature
line right up:

the sunset fills
the valley's rift,

the perfect circle
of the moon,

these pillar trees
and domes of hills,

those mountains flanking
left and right

—soft symmetries I start to see
if I look past the jaggedness,

align myself with nature's ways,

then witness finer parallels
between my fingers,
every branch,

the sounds of water,
thunder,
wind,

the fissures
splitting bark
or stone,

more patterns:

marble,
clouds,
and bone,

the vascular canyons,
veins of caves,

the beach accepting
cresting waves

—vast natural geometries
convincing me how nothing here
is reasonless, completely chance,
an accidental happening.

Palliative

Assuaged abrasions.
Breaches mend.

Persistent fissures
narrow, close

now snow consoles
embattled lands:

the wind walks
gentle as a nurse
and swaddles earth
in bandage white
and pads
these tender hills
which wear
the silvery salve
of half-moon light.

Plush starry quilts
tuck in this sight.

At last,
the fractured
sleep tonight,

and

dreams of healing
gather height.

Snowpack

The mountains lay there lined up, cold and still,
like coffins draped with burial cloths of white,
but nothing can convince me they're deceased.

I've watched their subtle, slow, and silent work,
their patient days and months collecting snow,
devoted to their cause as gatherers
preparing for the coming springtime thaw,
when snowpack melts and water flows down slopes
to feed the river basins, glaciers, streams,
then lakes and all the thirsting world beyond.

I know how all this happens, yet I don't
dismiss these mountains as some lifeless rock.
They always seem much more to me—extant,
like Earth: sufficiently resourceful, keen
to lend the lands essential means for life
—survival, habitat, ecology.

Of course, it's physics: weather, gravity,
how life evolves around geology,
erosion, seasons—science through and through

—but I'll not minimize what mountains do
or credit chance with all their vital roles,
or go so far to say they have no souls.

Overcoming

The mountain knows of pressuring,

old welling stresses underneath
what once resembled peaceful fields,

which swelled and churned repeatedly
until those struggles ushered growth,

new heights above the ancient strain
to speak of toughness, tested strengths,
endurance over lesser things,

humility yet majesty
beyond all shards of fractured stone,
so mountain stands as more than rock,

much more than mass and aftermath
of unseen forces overcome:
it endures as our monument
of conflicts conquered and of time
defeated for a little while.

Sea Turtle Circles

Deposited in secret sand:

    one hundred eggs
    the mother turtle
    covers up
    and soon will strand.

Left on their own
    with no farewells,

    but with what basic instinct tells,

    the newborns chew
    and break through shells,

    then climb toward moonlight,
    into life.

Then desperate pressures rush at once:

    the race to reach the ocean's edge
    before they may become the prey.

The helpless hatchlings storm the froth,
    the crashing breakers,
    ruthless waves
    which likely lead to early graves.

There's no return,
   no burrowing,
   no shrinking from this crucial test
   when, sadly, few outlive the rest.

Adrift,
   submitting to the flow,
   they've little say
   where they will go.

Now water rules their hours, days,
   and few decisions will be made
   against the tide,
   the sharks,
   the dark,

so they press forward,
   feed or flee,

   then surface,

   breathe in,
   holding breaths,

  again,
    again,
      again,

        again
        back at the depths

where life might last
a decade or a century

or vanish unexpectedly.

And some sea turtles might mature,
see land, dig sand,
leave eggs once more
and cover them,
then trust the sea
to pull life towards its destiny.

Utopia for Deer

Yawning fawns
awakening
step calmly from the underbrush.

Mother doe,
already up,
leans by her buck: they breathe in peace.

No rifle shocks.
No hunters crouch.
Here, life's untroubled, free from fear.

Finding Yourself in the Universal Mirror

One evening,
you will turn

at last,

stare up

for once,

then understand:

you move not
"through the universe"

instead
YOU ARE THE UNIVERSE:

alive

as bright as comets, stars,

and whirling like those galaxies

with constellations all your own

and worlds within you yet to rise.

The cosmos moves throughout you, too,
affirming you're significant,

a facet of eternity
reflecting eons,
timeless light.

I pray you'll see this soon
some night.

Part Two

Enlightening

Like waterfalls:
    cascading
      sunlight
       saturates
       my eyelids,
       forehead,
       neck,
      and hair,
       each
      muscle,
       tendon,
      elbow,
       bone,
      then
       drenches
      every
     atom left
    and inundates
   my gasping soul,
  eventually enlightening
 my desolation, emptiness,
the sludge of time, so I might see
humility's lucidity, humanity's divinity.

Dawn after Storms

Floodwaters lapse to puddles here,
evaporating into mist
as sunlight filters through those gaps
of leaves dislodged by choppy winds.

It's August, more than midway through
this year of one too many storms,
and there's been little time for rest.
We sweep debris, regroup once more:

the splintered fencing, branches down,
adornments toppled on the lawn,
the tilted birdbath, stones come loose,
glass cracked or smashed by heavy hail.

As many tempests test my faith,
I still believe the worst has passed,
today, and every broken thing
shall be restored or soon replaced.

Now morning light intensifies,
the mountain pushes through the clouds,
tenacious to return to life
and weather any kind of strife.

Date Palm (Phoenix Dactylifera)

I once heard of a date palm seed
that lasted for two thousand years
and germinated in the dirt
when planted not that long ago.

And something in that offered hope
—of what, I'm not exactly sure.

Continuance? Endurance? Love,
that renaissance beyond all death?

Then what of every seed of breath,
each word we've sown between these grooves:
this soft gray matter of the head?

May they return? Defy the dead?

Late summer: I'm still gardening,
recalling scores we've left unsaid.
Within our silent stubbornness,
did we surrender endlessness?

Can we emerge from ashen earth?
Conceive renewal? Slow rebirth?

I sigh your name to conjure you.
A cardinal darts through the view.

For Real

I've paintings of mountains, photos of roses,
books on gardens, three on trees,
as if to turn rooms inside out,
bring nature in this living space.

But all the long I had it wrong:
I really ought to walk outside,
knees deep in snow, caress the sun,
let wind mess up my careful hair,

not shy from ice but relish it,
then meet the river near its edge,
attend its crucial music, dance
as rocks and currents verge on verse.

I'm wandering by yards again,
amazed by branches, landing geese,
if just a glimpse of cardinals:
red streaks of life best seen for real.

Oak Noticing

Fantastic broke oak
(caught in limbs)
was jostled loose
by last night's storm.

At dawn,
I found it lying by
the rock garden and flowerbed:

   long withered arm

   detached from time,

gnarled fingers pointing toward the fir,

   suggesting words
     …or caveats
     …one last request
     …a farewell bid

—or did it name its chosen heir?
—declare some love?
—petition prayer?

Fresh questions branch off into sleep…

these roots of dreaming
reaching
deep….

Cloudscape

The sky commences from my feet
and spans the surface of the earth,

so, when you say, "You're in the clouds,"
it's true. I walk toward hurricanes,

roam overcast, breathe mist and fog,
watch cities choke on caustic smog,

trace contrails left by endless jets,
volcanoes blazing days away,

gold smolders of old holy wars,
sick billowings of industries,

dim heavens never fully glimpsed
since wildfires sear the night.

I've sensed an even deeper light
past vague rays of a straining sun:

the dawn of knowledge, newness, truth
beyond exhaust or darkening

—what must be noticed, not obscured
by any tragic atmosphere,

or lost to ambiguity.
I'll banish shadows till I see.

Libretto

Ascendant as an aria,
new butterflies sing with their wings,
impressing lyrics in the wind.

A billion voices join from cliffs,
from branches, dancing currents, dirt:
the existential opera swells

—elusive music few ears know
above our crass cacophony,
our dissonant oblivion.

Though overtures of life play on,
we seldom sense earth's orchestra,
its harmonies of endless keys

—as if we have no part in this
grand score of all creation's notes
progressing through eternity.

Curatorial Tutorial

The shores accept
whatever currents bring,
from driftwood, seaweed,
newly emptied shells
to starfish, fossils,
bones of whales aground.

Note how the shores take in
our rubbish, too
—our shipwrecks, cans,
old plastic ropes and wraps,
our spills and metals,
polished shards of glass.

It might appear
the beaches don't object,
but I maintain
these shores perform a role
as curators,
collecting what was cast,

revealing things
don't wholly sink away
—that they'll persist,
lend consequence, return,
and what's thought lost
exerts a presence yet.

Nuptials

Sky,
bridal white,
by altar earth:

    new marriage vows mix with the wind,
    which clears late leaves and carries seeds
    past what the widowed winter left.

Now, Time,
that anxious minister,
asks hurriedly if I will hold
this firmament of spousal light
from this day forth, for better, worse,
through wealth or poorness, illness, health,
as long as we exist

        —of course

    the only answer is, "I do,"
    since all of this is matrimony,
    weddings pledging life to lives,

part covenant of lungs to air,
to breathe, exhale, exchange, and share
in every seasoned moment hence,
then press ahead of mortal planes
to circle round devotion's cause:

from heart to hearts toward something more,
outside the forest of ourselves,

above horizons, surfaces,
roots overgrown, grand canopies,
the world of endings and rebirth,

to reach those realms celestial,
blend verve of earth with heavens, yes,
affirming, through fidelity,
angelic over mundane loves,
with blessings of continuance
toward sanctified vitality

—one chance to move beyond our will,
beyond the promises of years,
becoming closer to fulfill
this crucial union soon, until
these winds decline and clocks go still.

Rubato

The countryside appears untouched
by winter's interruptive slump:

unstirred, the spruce and birch abide
as rabbits pad about the knoll
near hyacinth which never left.

The meadow, did it even age?

Those boulders, so dependably
withstanding many months of snow,
they weigh like mighty paperweights,
preventing wind from scattering
unfinished verses of the earth.

Now clouds hang still as paintings, too.

I've relished this consistency
since rattled and sporadic days
unsettled years of calendars
until these recent peaceful weeks.

It's not that I'm against the change.

Of course, the woods grow as I breathe,
when no leaf stirs and limbs seem fixed,
suspended in another time.

I know the mountain inches forth
and underneath the sleeping rock
the restless worms renew the soil.

I've learned how stasis spreads decay,
that evolution cannot stay
if anything's to find its way.

The butterflies instruct me yet,
as do the icebergs, waterfalls,
volcanoes waking from the past,
the lunar phases, seasons, love.

I think to pause the vaulting world,
freeze meteors or words mid-flight,
keep hour hands from midnight's grasp,
prolonging measures of my song,
hold closing notes from tapering.

But life is motion, music. Sing!
To move along means everything.

Carrion

More crows and hawks detect the putrid scent
as do voracious vultures further out.

The flies and worms were already at work,
returning matters to receptive earth.

Soon larger darker wings will orbit it,
this crumpled creature in the sunken grass.

These birds of prey take time, descend in waves
upon the frayed remains until it's done,

when death becomes the utter sustenance,
what brings an end back to continuance.

And all these circles they'll fly through the sky
forebode the final curves toward stillness, peace,

consuming but to be consumed at last:
the awful feast that feeds the sacred rest.

Recipe for Mass Extinction Number Six

Polluted waters, wreckage, waste.
Resources, habitats erased.

Broken food chains. Oil slicks.
Greenhouse emissions. Politics.

Overfishing, coral bleaching.
Enterprises overreaching.

Warming, hunger, urban sprawl.
Deforestation. Vacant mall.

Obliviousness. Apathy.
Irresponsibility.

To a Crocus

Through snow you thrust
toward springtime light:

oh, crocus, yes,
you have it right:

to not be stopped
by what was dropped

but rise past ice,
old winter's woe,

revive and never
cease to grow!

Arboreal Time

The tree that keeps
   its leaves through fall
   depicts one wish:

sustain the sight
   of orchards, cornstalks,
   wheat, the sprawl
   of clover, ivy,
   crows in flight

before more orange,
   red, and gold
   dissolve when earth
   grows pale and cold.

Yet leafless trees
   feel more like me:

no longer hoarding
   or so caught
   by what must plunge
   toward history
   or sink beneath
   dead roots of thought.

Entangled branches.

Birth. Decay.

These woods divulge
  my mind today:

  relinquish seasons,

  rise past years,

  learn timelessness,
  what perseveres.

Breaching

Lost
thoughts
drift into
wishful waves,
swim inside
whirlpools,
undertow,
though
breaching whales
teach me
to fly,
escape
earth's weights,
engage
the sky,
romance,
go dance,
make way and play!

Coming to Light

Like loyal friends
    intent to intervene
    and keep me bright

    whenever melancholy
    turns a budding day
    to wilting night,

the plants remind me
    life must have its light

    —that I should seek the sun,
    gain strength,

    derive delight
    from overcoming gravity
    and practicing vivacity.

And, seeing them achieve such leafy vibrant height,
I'm most persuaded they have got it right.

Nature Retreat

"Metropolis" describes my mind
when everything's abuzz and rushed
as gridlock wits wait to advance
and crowds of concepts cross or pause
at every hectic intersection,
checking watches, headlines, signs
for progress, hope of going home.

It's there attention must retreat
from concrete curbs—the urban surge
of hurried thoughts—to seek the peace
and patient pace of nature's cure:
wide meadows loved by butterflies
and hummingbirds and wild blooms
which thrive outside all boundaries.

Then meditation may begin:
reflections spread across great lakes
embracing air, the gaping sky,
its gentle clouds of cushioned views,
where distance glistens limitless
and free horizons revive life
with saving rays of rising light.

Away

Between the chasm blurred by churning fog
  and one faint sign that warns of Falling Rocks,
    I pause with caution, check for evidence
    some ruptured stone becomes unsettled soon,
    dislodged from constancy, destabilized
        from eons of peace secured from warring times.

  Long jagged slants behind the sign reveal
  the peril's real: slabs of damaged earth
    lay prostrate, having stumbled far enough
to near that dreadful edge, where precipice
becomes the drop, the bottomless abyss
  which blindly receives every diving thing.

Today, there's little fear in standing here
  and squinting into sunless nothingness,
    since emptiness immerses all, it seems.
    But it's a trick perception likes to play
    with thoughts inclined to plunge in wonderment
        of schisms, healing, flawlessness, descent.

  Whatever pressures years of inner strength
    or fractures then disintegrates that mass
      and menaces the grand totality
    should move us to survey what lives or gives,
what love's enough to keep us whole and close,
away and safe from senseless plummeting.

Elsewhere in the Universe

While others
   clap at fireworks
as light shows
   scatter into smoke,

I stare
   into my telescope
and focus
   on the dimmest dot

—a star so far,
   so faint, though more
astonishing
   in ageless ways.

Plainspoken

The mountain seems to domineer,
though one lone pine stands in its way
as David faced Goliath once
with little cover, fragile arms,
yet something of a fearlessness.

But no stones will be launched today.
No giant shall be vanquished here.

The mountain's never perishing,
for there's no stand-off there or near,
no looming brawl or fall at all.

The feud's illusion versus truth,
imagination's clash with facts,
metaphor's war against the mundane

—life's conflicts with reality,
what poets hide or might not see.

Revival

I'm watching dogs play on the hill,
amused how each can dance and roll,
swerve sideways, bolt or chase, and pause
for seconds, then go back for more,
cavorting in their awkward sport
where there's no loss, no second place,
just bliss of speeding in this race
beyond a stopwatch, referee,
or any error's penalty,
like many of us did before
as children thrilled to crash the lawns,
spring headfirst into orange leaves,
storm puddles after summer rain.

Who gave much thought to shame or pain,
exhaustion, time, clean clothes, or fear?
Like these pups here, we'd love up life
without an ounce of doubt or strife
for such a brief but special while.

Now, somehow, benched in this green park,
I'm free to lean in peace and smile
as dogs rush Sunday, lark and bark.
Throughout these moments, I'm there, too,
alive, excited, old though new.

On High Point, New Jersey

I left my notebook home today
and kept the camera in its case
so I might stand still, clear this mind
to contemplate (impossibly)
this panorama three states wide,
from ceaseless trees to flaring blue
in all directions from my feet:

the Catskills and the Poconos
beyond the Kittatinny rise,
and, further out, the Delaware
unwinding most deliberately
through leafy banks of autumn woods
reflecting gently in the flow
of water blending land with sky.

I've scribbled notes, snapped photographs,
recorded sights, descriptions, thoughts,
but missed the true encountering,
whole revelations small or large,
those details vastly minuscule,
impermanence yet permanence
surrounding me, including me:

alyssum, outcrops, butterflies,
their frail ballet above the world,
this cloudscape paintings can't contain,

those furrowed hills of verdancy
more vital than my poetry,
and anything the senses miss.
So this is why I'm silent here:

to hear earth's verses, heed its arts,
be student more than audience
because I'll never learn enough,
observe, absorb, or know enough.
Between these ants and hidden crags,
I should see what exceeds my eyes
and listen close, not rhapsodize.

Part Three

Bedrock Awakening

These pebbles bedded in thick mud,
with all their varied hues and shapes,
have never always slept right there.

They've ventured quite a stretch for years
—for many, millions, others more—
chronologies beyond our books.

How easily they're overlooked,
bypassed as background elements,
although they tell essential tales.

Imagine what each one has known:
long ancient lakes, lost waterways,
the first of fires, dinosaurs.

I gather stones and wash them off,
inspecting fissures, sanded bands,
those details only eons carve.

Up close, each piece looms mountainous,
more mythical than modicum
within the confines of my palms.

More sagas surface everywhere:
the weathered epics of the earth,
adventures yet commenced or sensed

—and then my quest of life to write,
upon this yawning, breathing page
between the bedrock and the sage!

Peaceable Earth Beginning with Me...

I've tried to be
the leaf that finds
its due place
in the dewy earth
when finished spinning
into wind.

At times I'm rock
which rolls to close
an unfilled space
around the ground
long since it's tumbled
from some hill.

I hope to be
like rain or snow
which takes new forms
across the world
to rouse life after
ice or drought.

Outreach

I wanted to be mountainous
as Himalayas, paramount

—magnificence that rushed the skies,
astonishing unnumbered eyes.

But that is asking to be seen
from every angle, distance, time

—to be the standard—Everest!—

compared and dared throughout my days
once people come from everywhere
to size and climb, snap photographs,
reduce me to a bragging right,
their challenge, backdrop, trivia,

another "Wonder of the World"
commodified and posterized
or mythified and glorified,
appraised against all other things.

And, honestly, who wants all that?
(I do not ask the narcissists.)

I'm really closer to these hills:
they rise and dive much like my life,

ascending for a little while
before returning back to earth
to wallow where the willows tilt
and wildflowers burst and wilt
among the fields, fox, and deer,
and, further, past the river's lisp,
the plains between the pinnacles,
where certain goats and peregrine
have clawed expanses, lofty heights
above the summit of my mind.

It's in this humbler ground I find
more purpose than superlatives,
more betterment beyond "the best,"
more modest steps from brush to stream
and back to solid land on rocks,
who know no lesser magnitude
than any alps I fancied once:

they're all essential, meaningful,
components of momentousness
outreaching every one of us
and yet embracing everything.

Rewilding

Where we have
              trampled,
    crushed,
              disturbed,
    disgraced,
              displaced,
    debased,
              erased,

let us regret,
    redress,   replace,
    restore,   revive,
    redeem,   recede,

so what was wild,
    fertile,
    pure,

    recuperates,
    rejuvenates,

    reclaimed from ruin,
    gluttony,
    contamination,
    apathy.

Conserving nature's sanctity,
we preserve earth's vitality.

Human Natural

We're human, foremost, souled and fleshed
with sinew, hearts, and skeletons
on paths alive as life itself:

distinctly driven to exist,
instinctively in search of light,
biotic, though with artistry

—creators of creation's cause
proceeding out of deeper seeds
the heavens planted in this ground.

From cosmic loam, the soil of stars,
comes everything, runs everything,
stops everything, starts everything.

Let us acknowledge basic facts,
ingredients of elements
assembled here in special time,

and let us give thanks to trees, the sea,
that atmosphere so long prepared
so there could be this air to breathe.

Let us esteem ecology,
how organisms unionize
in habitats that work to thrive.

And let us really give a damn
when nature meets our negligence
or some endangered thing goes lost,

for human nature's life of life,
a yield of the dust and trust
from every growth endowed before.

Know human nature's all this land:
these mountains, meadows flourishing.
The planet's wellness is our own;

our lungs inhale its oxygen.
We feast on harvests, starve in deserts.
The earth bears life, brings sustenance.

These flowers of the day are us:
what blooms or wilts concerns us all.
Discount no petal. Love each leaf.

The Rapids vs. River Birch

When stressed, I think of riverbanks:

how rapids quicken turbulence,
accelerating during falls
once water flees.
escaping
peace

yet

river birch
live differently
with toleration, sustenance,
providing shelter, lending nests,
accommodating moths and birds

—surrendering,

benevolence,

then natural tranquility.

Said a Tree at Sycamore Canyon

It started there,
that wooded stretch,

the forest of a hundred trees,

upon a limb since left behind
a century or so ago:

the seed of me
whisked into wind,
delivered toward this residence
along the canyon's jagged slope.

What saplings choose their rooting ground?

This precipice invites distress
if all you'd witness is the risk
then covet firm dirt, lower lands,
the certainties of vapid plains.

Discerning seedlings between stones,
observe we flourish and have found
we'll overgrow where we were cast

—such truths we old trees testify:

we can survive, advance above,
and branch beyond the barren past.

Befriending Nature

Let's love the mountains,
lakes and trees,

the beaches, rivers,
skies and seas,

the pebbles, plants,
each form of life,

what suffers under
human strife.

Befriend the lions,
lambs, and snakes.

Let's treasure earth,
for all our sakes.

Great Egrets

With panoramic angel wings
spread feathery in heavenly light,

    the egrets return,
    one by one
    adorning the marsh
    awash with insects,
    frogs and fish

    —and also (they hope)
    receptive mates
    expecting nesting,
    courting dances,
    eventually
    the blessing of eggs

—the simplest things,
the most essential goals,
which will suffice to make
this modest plot of earth
their private paradise.

An Hour in the Life of a Snowshoe Hare

Endurance   blurring   equanimity.

Palpitations
under fur,

  though legs may rest,
  for now,

  for now.

For now
  the hunting bobcat's drained
    from zigzag chases
over snowfall.

  Now...

    complacence?

Vigilance!

Predation's everlasting here.

Survival means outleaping fear.

Consulting the Oak

An acorn
    falling
        starts it
         all:

         what
         carries on
         a line
         of life
         the moment
         that its
         taproot
         grows
         to be
         an anchor
         in this

         dirt.

    Then roots commence
   their lifelong quest
to gather water, nutrients,
which feed what will become the tree
  and send the cycle round again:

the trunk that thickens and divides
into the limbs that lead toward leaves

and clustered acorns swelled as fruit
which give to ground, to gravity,
or get dispersed by storms or stress
of searching squirrels, perching birds.

This falling
    pointing toward the rise
    comes down to base stability,
    those lateral roots spread out, ahead,
    in all directions several times
    the width of what we call the crown,
    the branches full of foliage.

In this way, I consult the oak
    and contemplate its vital might
    and ask again how strength evolves,
    how life could reach longevity
    and nurture durability,
    gain stamina against the wind,
    invigorate the earth and us
    to flourish with resilience,
    and let the small things

        be immense.

Vernal Equinox

I'll turn to any evergreen
to comfort me as seasons change
and suddenly it's somewhat strange
to shift from winter out of fall
or stare from summers back at springs.

While other trees give up their leaves
once numb November nears again,
the red pine, cedar, and the spruce
remain themselves, though they adapt
to weather what December brings.

They face age with a certain poise,
a strength I try I understand
but rarely care to emulate
whenever wind descends again
and day becomes a quest for heat.

Through frosting panes, I prize their nerve
against the cold and growing old,
their constancy reminding me
I should remember, not dismiss
the blizzards before vernal bliss.

Entwining Light

My eyes leap freely,
star to star,
  like summer children
  wonderstruck
in wooded yards
of August sun
  cascading through
  the dancing leaves,
where every stunning
thing I see
  excites my mind's
  astronomy,
connecting forests,
galaxies,
  eternity, the earth,
  and me.

While Shoveling

The blizzard's finished with its funeral,
and, after one more silent pause, I move
to dig the driveway from its wintry tomb.

Amid the mummified trees, the plastered cars,
and frosted fences holding little back,
the ghostly snowdrifts shroud the rocks and all.

One trifling patch of blacktop slowly grows
with every heavy pass of shoveling.
At least these stars are starting to return.

Now evening contrasts with this frozen earth,
though progress seems all but impossible
while time and temperatures descend again.

I find I'll never clear the drive tonight;
beyond this, knowledge runs as sparse as stars:
sporadic facts among a thousand doubts.

I know the Wednesday forecast calls for rain.
Two cups of cocoa will be stirred and sipped
beside my wife, before our glowing hearth.

We'll chuckle, snuggle soon, become the warmth
that saves this world from turning into ice
and makes the bleakest season paradise.

To the Full Moon

Full moon eclipsing human lights,
no neon, billboards, passing jets
distract our eyes from you tonight:

at last that stellar stage is yours,
and you are Carmen, Tosca, yes,
Queen of the Night, or Butterfly,

whose arias enrapture us
attending every lunar truth
you sing into our silent lives.

You're Violetta, vexed with love,
as long your songful strains remain
and all that fades is time or pain.

Floriculture

You've gathered flowers
    in your hair

curated bouquets,

pressing petals
    in your diaries

       but

will you dance
    like daffodils?

shine like asters?

love like roses?

climb like lotus,
    high, toward light?

Rendering

Gray lanes divide bright lands in half
   and perforate horizon lines.

Gold flowered fields gleam then cease
   where pavement rolls until it bends
   and greenery may breathe again.

One forest becomes two or more
   so highways might reside here, too,
   with painted margins, miles marked.

Of course, we need to make our ways,
   to travel, work, raise homes, and live.

We order earth to step aside,
   and nature always seems to give
   yet holds no grudge and still provides.

Now cracking roads are fading fast.
How much of this was meant to last?

Stems

I think of lotus, lavender,
wisteria and water lily,
milkweed and magnolia,
admiring their unique blooms,
how each seeks sunlight, open sky,
and knows the urgency of earth.

Beyond distinctions, surface hues,
roots draw from universal dirt,
communicate a commonness,
the most holistic unity
of entities, equality,
the concert of ecology.

They forego xenophobia,
see difference apolitically
because they need to tolerate,
adapt, advance, collaborate.
Whatever thrives cannot resist.
So plants share land. Fish coexist.

Life illustrates prosperity
can stem from this community.

Crystalline

My mother lives on in the amethyst,

the rose quartz or the orange tiger's eye,

this broken geode crystallizing light,

when I recall that academic set
of rocks and polished gems with minerals
so clearly labeled in that lidded box

—my seventh birthday present she gave me,

when summer was thick grass and gardens dug
with purposed fingers probing stones to free,

green seasons no one spoke of health or death,
except to eat your vegetables and watch
for cars whenever you go biking past
the peony swarmed by bumblebees and ants,
who search for nectar then depart when hours
arrive at last to move ahead once more

—like now, while purple dusk becomes bold stars,
whose gifts of clarity redeem the void.

Notices

One wish walks with me where I go:
to notice something I've not known,
a quantity or quality,
perhaps an action, sight or sound,
an unheard bird, a sudden scent,
new paw prints pressed in sodden earth,
strange rhythms skipping in a brook,
the markings on a squirrel's tail,
or how the rusted hinges sing
in different keys from week to week,
and if the furthest fir tree seems
to lean a little left or right,
with all its needles, thick and flat,
revealing cones in wild wreaths
the wind unweaves and weaves again.
Whatever detail I might find
is one more diamond in my mind.

Audience

I may not notice where the flies
were gathering this afternoon,

or how the squirrel hid his nut,
or when the monarch cleared the fence,

or why the pine cone's in this path,
or which finch scattered half the bath.

Like them, I live this little life,
and much slips by my scrutiny,

but then I'll watch the watchful deer
from kitchen windows as they graze,

observe unnerving swerving hawks,
bright dragonflies, their flashing wings,

the howling crows and frantic ants,
the dancing grass betraying snakes.

I should be mindful, more aware
as three more geese leap toward the air.

See how the maple's reddening!
Come hear the owls start to sing:

their questions serenade my night
above the crickets out of sight.

Part Four

Kindred of the Earth

I love the chipmunk,
doe, and fox,

the oak and maple,
fern and phlox,

the hungry woodchuck,
cautious mouse,

the snake that slithers
past the house,

the finch, the squirrel
on its spree.

They're not just friends,
they're family.

At One's Disposal

Imagining: to be that tree,

    the one cut
    down,

    so young,
    undone.

How high
and wide it might have stood

    with leaves of gold,
    deep reaching roots,

    strong branches
    home to woven nests.

Instead, it's toppled, overgrown,
unfit for timber, firewood,

    though home to mice who do not know
    this forest will be cleared today

    so we'll have more convenience stores,

    another place to get our gas

        to drive those roads
        yet to be
        paved.

Weather Proof

These starless hours ruled by rain
cannot obstruct the coming sun,

the drive of life's imperative
anticipating radiance,

the revelations of the rays
unshadowing the things we lost,

whatever wind absconded with
as thunderbolts secured our eyes,

and that which nighttime did disguise
or draped in shades of mystery.

Seek testimony in these blooms,
in every thing grown green and far:

these leaves and weeds, the grass and trees
affirm the darkest days shall pass,

that earth returns bright mountainsides
with changed terrain and shifting tides,

young birdsong, bees, new lunar moths
emerging soon from cool cocoons.

The clouds of doubt float powerless,
dissolving while we brace with faith,

let patience raise our silent might,
and weather what eclipses light.

Canadian Wildfire Smoke in New York City
June 6, 2023

Some several hundred miles on,
a funeral without a wake:
succumbing before summer's run,
as thousands others passed today,
another tree turns into flames,
its particles strewn by the wind
like ashes of a loved one cast
from land to water by worn hands.

How helpless Lady Liberty
stands with her lantern gripped on high
while smog engulfs her island, chokes
the city of its clarity.
We barely breathe, though we might see
how distant death drifts everywhere,
can even reach beneath concrete,
from skyscrapers down to the street.

Ten thousand trees have died to show
remoteness offers no defense
against the spread of suffering:
what happens elsewhere hits us here,
behind these panes, these stories that
may seem to say we stand apart
from everything beyond, below.
Now smoke's within us, we should know.

Arches National Park

Majestic etched memorials:

long arching rocks beyond the gorge
embrace sublime antiquity
while blazoning the ages here
with verging curves encircling
the permanence of worldly turns.

Bright vaulted stones arc heavenward,
exalt the sky with faithful grace,
a selfless reach toward sacred space
appropriately brimmed with light.

Broad elemental windows rise:

they beckon us to share their news,
then ponder earth, its openness,
and live to love those lordly views.

Before a Minimalist Landscape

Elusive alpine majesty,
ahead and yet impossible
to cram in narrow canvases,

much like these monumental pine
around the water: life outgrows
and flows beyond a landscape's frame.

I sense this artist has it right,
conveying shapes expressively,
relieved of details far too fine:

no needles, cones, or crackled peaks
or faint gradations gracing clouds
or trifling ripples through the lake

—no lavish bids to duplicate
the dappled banks or battered crags,
the pleated slopes or mottled bark.

To live the rest, we must stand there,
absorbing nature's teeming arts
until the mountains burst our hearts.

Sakura Selflessness

When cherry blossoms reach full bloom,
their final week of flowering,
what do they do? They give.

They give.
They live.
They give
and give,

endowing pleasures, memories,
bold symbols of renewal, hope,
grand metaphors of life and time
—yet, once their budding season ends,

they still give
live,
and live
to give,

bestowing petals to the air
with no delay, dismay, despair,

until each floral branch goes bare
and beauty's bequeathed everywhere.

A Prayer for the Squirrel

I pray for you,
adventurous friend

 —how you
   dodge traffic,

hide
 from
  hawks,

   abandon
     branches,
 outwit owls,
foxes,
 snakes,

  then risk
    existence
      for
      one
      nut.

Leap peacefully.
Sleep well tonight.

Diamond Reflections

The diamonds dug up from the earth
look nothing like those precious stones
we'll see on rings or royal crowns.

The real ones don't glow at first
and won't emerge as beautifully
as most of us suppose they'd be.

They're coarse, uncut, sunk underground,
quite hidden from the upper world,
reached only through persistent work.

Before this, for some billion years,
they form in darkness, pressuring,
exceptional degrees of heat.

When I surmise my life is rough,
I ponder diamonds, what it takes
to make and shape each masterpiece,

—the measuring and polishing,
the pleasure of endeavoring
toward facets that embrace the light—

and I know I must strive, persist,
resolve to be more diligent,
if I'm to shine as half as bright.

Travel Magic

Four hundred plus kilometers
from everything considered home,
I'm dwelling in discovery,
a study of comparisons:

this sky that rises higher, brighter,
denser woods spread further, dark.
That alder, pine, and chestnut bark
seem utterly impeccable

while streams careen with purposed verve,
as do the robin, lark, and crow.
When I confront the routine rose,
it's redder than remembered, yes

—arrangements stranger, alien,
revealing angles, aspects, more
in things I've should have seen before,
since it's the same world past that door.

But this is travel's magic now,
a newness cast upon old eyes
intent on staying curious,
beguiled by familiar things.

And so I play the visitor,
enchanted by disarming charms,
in awe that disappears too soon
behind the specters of our years.

On the Nature and History of Influence

Examine how sea waves emerge,
converge, diverge,
submerge,
resurge.

Too much?

Observe
one water drop:

where
did it start?

Why
might it stop?

The Rocks Remembering

The rocks are Earth's discreet historians,
collecting volumes of our days and deeds,
transcribing subtle matters of the wind,
archiving seasons, all the waters, land
in what we plainly call geology.

For me, these rocks have been much more to us:
they're steadfast watchers, conscious guardians
protectors of the ancient memories
along with all the present happenings
and major changes every age has faced.

Why would they gather—for many billions of years—
such details small as dust and even less?
Perhaps the rocks expect us to forget,
and they'd be right: just look at what we've lost
between the hours, today, the week before:

how little we will manage to recall,
so focused on our trivia—or caught
by fleeting flashes that distract our sight
from mindfulness, its peace of memory.
And this is how the rocks defend our world:

through purposed strength, resolve no armies found,
with mountains, boulders, canyons, lava, crags,
and every chip and pebble underfoot
securing bits of past, so heirs of earth
receive these clues and learn their lasting truths.

To the Woods of Livelihood

Your roots:
our home.

Your limbs:
our arms.

Your leaves:
our hands.

Your crowns:
our heads.

You breathe
our breath.

Your sky's
our mind.

You fall,
all fall:

one earth
entwined.

Forty Minutes on the Mountain

Up here, about the mountaintop
peace meets my every compass point,
and I may breathe, exhale with ease,
and pause before the sprawling world,
abstracted from barbarity,
that random pandemonium
exiling us from paradise.

I think of Moses, of the call
to climb toward heaven and receive
commandments in the form of stone
—directions clear, indelible,
divinely rendered, ageless phrase
to lead one's people out of night.
It's sinful not to share this sight.

I wish I could descend these slopes
with wiser verse encouraging
a love of something less than gold,
devotion worthy of this earth,
this hallowed ground where bushes burn
and sacred life's round every turn,
if only we would search and learn.

Said

A robin pauses,
chirps at me.

Gratitude for seeds,
perhaps?

The birdbath cleaned?

Imagining
shared words with birds…

conferring daily with a tree

—I wonder what
life's said to me.

Inaudible

Though all seems silent,

    forests lecture,

    rivers preach,

    the mountain expounds.

Whatever we won't comprehend
says nearly nothing
of this world.

If We Are Stardust

If flesh is stardust
born again,
why aren't we
the radiance?

What is it we've
not gotten right?

Astronomy
instructs us some.

The heavens might
illuminate
if we'd be pupils
of their light.

Quenched

I drink the Hudson River up
with arid eyes, a soul so parched
for all the waters have to give,

and, in this way, I start to live,
revitalized by waves of light,
the rippling of the infinite

with seagulls of inspiriting,
which lift me as I simply stare,
swill in these currents, sip at air,

my senses never quenched for good
because there's been too long a drought,
too many seasons scorched by doubt.

I'll let this river in and wait
until it bears my cares away
and I drift forth for one more day.

Openness

Between these skyward canyon walls
carved hard by rivers out of time,
how can I count my meager weeks
or groan about my getting old
when decades mean so little here?

Chronology, that's for these rocks,
their plodding longhand chronicles
of cracks detailing centuries,
whole sagas of the measureless
—what I see now as timelessness.

I face the chasm, more aware
how canyons come from what's not there
—events, not years, defining life,
significance no age erased:
this openness to be embraced.

To a Blue Spruce

Blue Spruce, you root me firm in earth,
remind me I should rise, expand,
be true, myself, unique to see,
not green as every other thing.

You say, "Face every wind with calm"
and "Winter mustn't hinder us."
Then I find solace in your strength,
your constancy, longevity.

Much deeper than your hardiness,
you teach me we might leave this world
more beautiful because we're here,
among the mountains and the deer,

alive as individuals,
yet bound, united by this ground,
this oxygen and vital light.
You show me growth means more than height.

Part Five

Fisheye Lens

Imagine once

    you are the fish

    (caught up in nets)

    (or on the hook)

then

    pulled above
    with hundreds more.

Imagine life

    before and after:

    from the ocean
    to the dish.

Interstitial

Like breath for music
    pressuring
the gap-filled valves
    and brassy tubes
of trumpets blasting
    abstract jazz,

new sunlight rattles
    flaxen clouds
and rustles woods
    with golden notes
that flash and blare
    through swinging leaves.

Between blue breaks
    of ice or night
or frigid stints,
    those blazing riffs
kick winters from
    this drumming heart

    if I recall
    the song is life

    then sense red echoes
    fill the still.

Save

You yearn for "better worlds"

—again:

>   unsullied planets,
>   flawless air,
>   pastures,

sweeping wakeful flowerbeds,

somewhere you're regarding stars

>   and

cherished for your stellar worth.

Keep dreaming…

>   or…

help rescue Earth.

Muted

By stilling waters, birch trees lean
as if transfixed, if they had eyes
reflecting on their mirrored selves,
like dimmed Narcissus, blind to life
and everything—above all, love.

Somehow it's up to us to see
beyond these mythic tendencies
—romantic readings of the real—
so we might mind more muted truths
and moderate this vanity.

Look how these leafy beings swell
without a gasp of arrogance
or metaphors unheard, unloved,
gone lost behind those bright white blooms
inclined against our silent tombs.

Touching Textures

The earth runs neither smooth nor rough throughout,
and we can learn this from the smallest rocks:

   try tracing fingers over random stones,
   their fractures, ridges, cavities and rims,
   the brush of unexpected jaggedness,
   sleek surfaces that scarcely undulate.

Peer past veneers beneath the microscope
or magnifying glass. Discover veins,
concealed caverns, motley clouds between
the shimmering scintillas kissing light.

And so this holds for love and softer things,
like expectations, flesh, red velvet thoughts,
what's solace versus raw, silk memory,
diaphanous that answers ruggedness

   —depressions, hollows,
   scratches, spikes, and strife:
   sense every texture
   pressed against your life.

The Careful Hare

From under brush, the hare peers out,
sniffs at the air, deliberates
on what's ahead, above, behind
with widest eyes and shifting ears
attending every slightest sound
beyond its heartbeat and its breath.

Here, unawareness asks for death:
descending talons, piercing beaks,
the gnash of fox or famished wolf
or bear preparing for the freeze.
Though winter nears, there comes no rest.
Existence is an endless test:

to listen, heed, blink less than twice,
stare everywhere and audit all
before advancing into chance,
toward threats unseen, unheard, unknown
—the silent lynx high on the branch,
the eagle eyes between the clouds.

The hare lives in this vigilance
like many other creatures do,
unable to ignore the crunch,
what might be wind or diving wings,
coyote ambush, weasel teeth,
the bobcat panting, instant chase.

The hare sneaks forward, turns again,
protected by a blend of fur,
dead leaves, more shadows, weathered bark.
Now nighttime means the day begins:
nocturnal searches, foraging,
and care to meet another moon.

Crop Rotations

One farmland out of many crops:

> tomatoes climb where carrots grew
> until the beans and cabbage sprout,
> preceding parsley, celery,
> potatoes, peas, then radishes.

Variety revives the earth,
this soil that mustn't turn to dust
—that, year by year, opposes blight,
depletion, stasis, barrenness.

From acres off, it's a pastiche,
the variegation chance would plant,
until we gather, stand there, see
how everything now hinges on
these lavenders and leafy greens,
red stripes and bands of blue and white
by motley harvests, orange, gold,
sweet fruited hues and auburn hills
collecting lemons, plums, and peach:

> one country sprung from sundry yields
> sustaining change preserving growth
> that's nurtured in this difference

> —this flourishing diversity
> we cultivate,
> must celebrate.

Moonflowering

Another sunset's underway,
suggesting day has met its end,
but something's starting in the dark,
convinced this is as opportune
as afternoon to flourish, bud,
exhibit beauty even as
so many eyes grow heavy, shut.

This is the Flower of the Moon
or Morning Glory of the Night,
the nonconformist of the yards
whose buds defy old protocols
most other plants obey by day
—a vine that climbs in spite of all
we've reckoned as conventional.

Well after midnight, while I write
some verse that burgeons finally,
I'm mindful of the kinship here
between me and my lunar friend
—and how clocks wither, meaningless,
where progress can pass second hands
to reach a prime epiphany.

This hour's ripe for gardening
and gathering new blooming truths,
more nectar meanings outside time.

Bright petals rise against the void:
let nothing govern poetry
to sleep, be silent, wait for dawns,
especially when it bears light.

Earth for a Day

Envision being planet Earth...

serenely marble blue and white.
encircling your sun, the glows
of moon and starlight further out.

You're magma, water, land, and sky.
and, every day, new life appears
—so many creatures everywhere:

whole flocks of birds above your clouds,
long schools of fish below your waves,
the countless beings in-between.

You're dressed in mountains, valleys, lakes,
volcanoes, forests, rivers, streams,
grands canyons, deserts, islands, plains.

You have your seasons, continents,
your longitudes and latitudes,
degrees and time zones, dawns and dusks.

Alive at least four billion years,
you boom with earthquakes, ice, and storms.
Your rains can cleanse, relieve, or flood.

You're joined by siblings: Venus, Mars,
plus Pluto, Saturn, Jupiter
and others dancing past the light.

You move throughout the Milky Way,
your galaxy, your cosmic home,
and you're uncommon, as globes go,

though humans can forget that fact,
polluting and consuming what
you've gathered, crafted, and arranged.

You've seen the solar system changed
and witnessed comets, meteors.
You've frozen over, thawed, evolved.

You've known disasters, tragedies,
the mortals climbing toward their falls,
their needless wars and suffering.

You've watched their rockets, satellites,
the astronauts and billionaires
ascending and returning home.

You still remember dinosaurs,
old tribes and truths reduced to dust,
the artistry turned artifacts.

You've noted progress, great mistakes
repeated for millennia,
the punishments for ignorance,

delusions of the gullible,
deception, greed, and apathy,
oppression, hatred, vanity.

To be Earth is an endless cause,
an honor, burden, or a curse
since sleeping is prohibited,

though you know life depends on you,
what's here and what could soon arrive,
and thankless unseen works to do.

You've questioned every inch of this:
the reasons for your universe,
the purposes of whirling worlds.

Now, as a human, ponder on
what eons brought before your eyes
—perspectives in this exercise:

what do you see or realize?

Luna Moth

Once
  wings
    arrive,
      you've
        nights
         to fly,
           pursue
             light,
             thrive,
             chance
             dance,
             and
             glance
           at
         love's
       rushed
     life.

To the Stars

Too many eyes now slight your light
or view you as you never were,
as constellations, figured myths,
depictions since antiquity
of ancient names, forgotten tales,
dead legends, verses, patterned maps,
old scrolls of long-lost reference points
for captains, dreamers, oracles.

Tonight, I find it's just as well
I cannot tell Andromeda
from Perseus or Pegasus.
I'll see you as you really are,
no metaphors or telescopes.
Just optic nerve and universe,
your photons in these retinas,
pure energy to be received.

Squirrel for an Afternoon

For just some hours I'd be a squirrel,
bristling tail, thick fur, and all,
instinctive, quick, quite unabashed,
not thinking once before I'd launch
from lofty branches toward a trunk
then scurry earthward (upside-down)
and cross a frantic avenue
with little doubt I'd reach the oak
of falling acorns luring me
with dreams of lavish winter hoards
while hounds behind their chain-link fence
would growl and yowl hysterically.

I'd keep this to a noon, no more,
because I love the ground, this floor,
and much prefer these calmer days.
I leave the squirrels to their ways.

Imperative

I study earth with so much urgency
and often verge on sheer bewilderment
when news reports show old woes unresolved:

another river riddled with debris,
another species nearly gone extinct,
another forest scorched or lost for good.

Anxiety churns within then turns to words,
but when will verse alone become enough
to countermand the tragic vanishing?

I pray great poems burst free from my heart:
a billion butterflies to bear their light
toward every darkened soul that shuns the world

—but we need doers, action, even more:
compassion and cooperation, faith
in betterment and metamorphosis

—and will to climb above our crawling lives,
transform, and leave this chrysalis, then grow
to know and love the life past suffering.

Unbeknownst

What started as a hairline crack
(exacerbated by the wind)
becomes the fracture

  —soon,
   collapse:

     another bough's about to fall

   and with it
     many leaves and buds.

Now this shall go unnoticed, too,
  like most events we miss today
  because we live preoccupied
  with other things we scarcely see

  —attention being like that branch:
  dividing and diverging high
  from roots of thought once fixed in cause,

  before the split,
the splintering,

    the sinking feeling,

    then
    the fall.

Considering the Cows

I do not question if they think,
for cows exude serenity,
the peace deep contemplation brings
from open fields, skies, and eyes.

Now, cows are grouped with "ruminants,"
fermenting clover, clumps of hay
in vaster stomachs that extract
more nourishment than we ingest.

Yet cows are more than pasture, grass.
I gather they have grazing brains
and chew over life's mysteries
as natural philosophers.

Don't doubt they walk with views and truths
through existential inquiries
between the barnyard and the range,
the shambles and their sense of bliss.

From dawn to dusk, outdoors and spared
long fits of human lunacy,
these cows have days to ponder nature,
selves, and all—more so than us,

as we speed past the natural
and seldom pause to speculate,
or seek retreats, vacated scenes
where we may breathe and ruminate.

Part Six

Planting Marigolds

My mother spoke of marigolds,
new life behind the perished blooms,
how she could bring these flowers back,
then poured their seeds into my palms.

"They look like brushes, little brooms,"
I noted when I studied them,
those tiny black and brittle sticks
with dry white bristles slightly splayed.

She taught me how to sow them there,
just under soil, so they'd grow,
and this is how our garden sprouted
many, many Junes ago.

At times, I'll see some marigolds
then recollect those greener days,
the blossoming that follows death,
these seeds of hope we strew through life.

Continuous

I've tried in vain to trace the ocean's waves,
to seek where they begin, then crest and end,
and twice I thought I had it, long ago,
as combers foamed, two waves emerging fast
at different times in discrete ways, it seemed,
like whales arising from their briny depths,
not breaching but just surfacing to breathe,
then plunging back to darkness, peace, such leagues

beyond my dives and all my probes to know.

But then I saw it's all continuous,
these oscillations, climbs, subsiding life
epitomized by water here and everywhere:
how soon this looks to start and cease and surge,
immerse and disappear for good, although
the sea and we are one beyond the tides
—a constancy not plumbed enough when we
obsess on edges, shreds, the dangling strands
of tapestries unfurled past touch or time.

To the Manatees

My floating gentle restful friends,
sweet gurus of serenity,

   I see you drifting in your ease,

      forgoing time,

         unwinding,

           slow,

              no woes of weight
              or width
               or height.

You show us how kind
life might be
if we'd espouse
tranquility.

Scales

The realm of ants exceeds our world.

I know because I crawled with them
across the lawn, behind our house.

We moved by inches—fast for us,
when yards were miles, clover trees,
and pebbles rose like boulders there.

I understood immensity,
the eminence of little things.

And then I was an elephant,
a whale one time, then a giraffe.
Our world seems smaller through their eyes,

these titans of the earth and sea
who loom and leap at larger scales
and easily could trample us.

I recognized the minuscule,
what giants bypass, cannot glimpse

—and that this middle ground we tread,
from quarks toward atoms past the stars,
is something to appreciate.

See, we possess the lenses now,
the microscopes and telescopes
to watch beyond the medium

—and we've invented instruments
to weigh and pace and calculate
these differentials everywhere.

Now earth's the dot, the universe,
blue rounded rock of river time,
or something somewhere in-between:

it's how and when you choose to zoom,
what I decrease or magnify,
and where we dare to quantify.

I'm sure because I've thought of God.

Progress

The rocks know water always wins,
will infiltrate the thinnest cracks
and wear the fiercest edge away
through subtle motions over time,
for decades or for centuries,
as long it takes to smooth a grove
or to remove an obstacle
which blocks the progress cosmic laws
have shown must flow most naturally
from high to low and there to here.

So water courses sheer and clear
decisively, without delay
from day to week to month to year,
no matter what the rocks may say.

Craft

Artisan winds and waters work
for ages as they sculpt the stones,
subduing edges, hollows, peaks,
refining details down to grains
the eons only bring to us.

I've tried to keep that firm in mind
while kneading gray unyielding clay
to coax it from a block or blob
toward something far more definite
—a face, volcano, mountain, cloud.

Most efforts end in humbled clumps,
awareness of my ignorance,
so now I study currents, skies,
unhurried rainfall, easy streams
and learn from their deliberate craft.

Against Noise Pollution

A scurry of seagulls flee their sleepy beach
as speedboats cleave and veer before the shore.

A startled fawn escapes its father's side
and runs from rumbling garbage trucks again.

Another summer concert thunders into dusk,
its tremors sent through forest, rock, and sky.

An engine spurns engaging melodies
the nightingales propose with all their soul.

It's difficult envisioning a time
when only nature's voices spoke or sung.

Now, who could hush these rushing years
crescendoing without an end in sight?

Not me, though I should ease my deeds and see
our planet suffers all we've said and done,

and one upheaval, clank, or bang, or clash
can plague existence unexpectedly.

Let us move soundly, love the lulls, and choose
to save some quietude and peace each day.

Towards a More Natural Meditation

I'm meditating by the lake.

Loud wind goes silent.
Currents still.

The sky runs cloudless.
Leaves sleep well.

The sunlight's easy.
Clarity's near.

I'm concentrating on my breath:

inhaling long,
exhaling slow,

soft cyclic rhythms,
lungs to lips,

in lips toward lungs,
smooth breathing, free.

My pulse winds down. The lost hush comes

—until a crucial goose careens
into the water's looking-glass,

wide shock waves rippling outward quick
as awkward wings create a wake.

The goose floats off quite quietly
with greater poise, more dignity,

such that I start refocusing,
vacating thoughts, regaining calm

—until nine other geese arrive
and crash and honk and plash at length.

My gut reaction says to leave,
seek understanding elsewhere fast,

especially now more geese come
and clamor, splashing as they wish.

I watch them waft and fan across
reflections fizzed and dizzying.

I'm almost entertained, abstract,
forgetting what I walked here for:

to leave commotion, flee the sprawl,
escape to nature, clear my mind.

The more I watch, though, I'm spellbound,
deliberating on their ways

—the fact they just flew north again,

and that this is how they exist,

without delay, excuse, or doubt,
yet with the seasons' vital time

—and, honestly, this is their land.
Unlike them, I'm the visitor

—their interruption, if I move,
endanger their tranquility.

And so I sit. I watch. I learn
as several dozen geese return.

Their blare, it's not the city's din,
the human churning of machines;

it's nothing we should label "noise,"
some uninvited grating sound:

this is their language, music, verse.
I can't deny their poetry.

In ruminating on these truths,
I'm meditating once again

—not of, or for, or by myself,
but with—and for—this living earth,

whose peace is neither lifelessness
nor arid silence by the lake.

These natural acts that plunge and ring,
they move me toward more tolerance:

to welcome geese—all nature's themes—
with love for life, what sings and teems

—then let my meditation be
the peace I reach through empathy.

Sandstone

The tale of sandstone's the story of all:

    how trillions of particles
    for millions of years
    disperse
    then travel,
    settle,
    bind

    as more than remnants,
    sediment,

    becoming things above the dust,

    with contributions from old stone,
    the winds and waters,
    gravity,

    slow gatherings,
    long weathering
    all captured in this patterned rock,
    whose textures tell us of the past.

And Earth works like this,
    as we do,
    like stars
    and every cosmic thing:

scintilla masses magnitude.

Once ancient causes craft
  what was.

Now matters shall disintegrate,
  returning fragments to create
  the soul of something new,
  unique.

Effortless

Still heron by the teeming stream,
you seem reflective, quiet, calm,
so stately yet exempt from means

—more meditative than I'd be
when I search for serenity
then find myself preoccupied
with business elsewhere, memories.

It must be mostly effortless,
as clear as water to you, yes,
this life I tend to overthink.

Existence could be free as flight,
instinctive, boundless, natural,
not fraught with obstacles, restraints,
the pressures of possessions kept.

You thrive beyond such weighty things
—that's how you can soar off, away,
wherever you would turn at will,

while I rush homeward, check missed calls,
review to-do lists, overlook
the easy beauty of this earth.
Without one word, you teach me peace.

Rain Gauging

Whatever rains collects
inside my hands

begins as single droplets
interspersed,

which then connect and swell
into this pool,

which soon will overflow,
exceed my grasp,

descending unto earth,
absorbed again.

The rest runs off, collecting
somewhere else,

and gathers elsewhere till
the flooding comes

or rainfall culminates,
and wet goes dry.

And this is how our tears
collapse in time,

with sorrow spreading out
towards joy or silencing.

Autumn in Reverse

Brown leaves emerged
from brittle
sleep

becoming yellow
orange
red

and
next

ascending

one

then all

restoring
August

summer

spring:

deep
greens
awaken
every thing.

Part Seven

Soil of Life

What nourishes our verdant world?
Why all this humus underfoot?
I wondered much before I learned
how nature nurtures, purges, stays.

The answers would amaze me so:
it's nothing short of everything,
what weds the living with the dead,
erosion, growth, and weathering,

then seasons, ages, layered change,
the particles of rocks and bones
blown wide and far, collecting here
in what looks like just clumps of dust,

this matter of life's magnitudes,
where waters mix with minerals,
organics, sand, and clay with silt
and microscopic life that feeds,

then mulch, the waste of animals,
these nutrients reviving dirt
—consumption turned to sustenance,
as crops supply our harvests reaped.

I'm still astonished how these things
will yield seeds, then branches, grass,

devoured fruits of hungering,
these crumbled bits that gather mass

for hidden worms in cyclic grounds,
accumulations and decay
maintaining means from death to birth:
what resurrects this urgent earth.

Original Liberty

The very first birds
weren't born
indoors

    because

what flies
will only thrive
outside,

embracing nature

    (never
     walls)

through open instincts,

individual will,

and widespread wings
above the unobstructed country,
which only total liberation brings.

Lineage

Our lineage lives in this earth,
below the muddled understory,
meshed with roots, prime trees of time,
the offspring of those first few seeds
embracing ancient rain and rays
for generations, countless springs
in fields birthed of fire, ice,
then flooded, drained, revitalized
before we sprouted into thought
and sought to speak of heritage.

Now each tree is my family tree.
With cousin streams and sibling hills,
I stride beside my father's sky,
my mother's land, the sea, my wife,
and everything descends from stars,
this living loving universe,
where physics lists our origins,
our cosmic singularity,
regardless of how far we'll go.
The mountains? Kin. This much I know.

Neighborly

Though nowhere close,
we're neighbors still:

    we share an address in this earth.

Our maps obscure
that basic fact

    —and yes, we lack community—

but what burns
half a world away

    leaves ashes here in our back yard.

No streets or states
divide our lives

    —such labels cannot separate

or pin us
to proximity

    —not when the globe grows smaller yet

and we must be
more neighborly.

More Intimate Cosmology

Know eyes desire darkness, ease,
release from burning branding signs,
from camera flashes, endless streams
from flickering distracting screens,
tall stories bleeding radiance,
all speeding beaming vehicles,
and any artificial glow
obscuring Venus, Mars, and night.

Escape the vagueness, barriers,
false fears of voids and mysteries,
the tutors who discouraged you,
whatever still prevents you from
approaching heaven's telescope.

Gaze outside ancient maps and myths
of constellations, satellites,
old names and numbered galaxies.
Let stars enlarge your earthly view.

Come see our perfect universe:
this everything including you.

Running with the Seagulls

A hundred startled seagulls rise,
return at once.

My heartbeats climb with them and then
descend again.

Gulls glide around and land as one,
displaced though calm.

I wish they could fly further, safe
along clean shores,

not in this grungy parking lot
of jagged stores.

To the Sky

Your
 nebulous now
   scrolls vaporous
 before,
behind,
   above our waking
         daybreak eyes
             anticipating radiance,

         the openness

             of cloudless
                 skies.

Tonight,
   horizons lie in haze
     as murky lines
       dividing time
   define the sunset from my rise
     of what should be
 tomorrow's light.

       So much you've shown me
 through my youth.

   So much you've taught me

all my years.

So much I've witnessed
in your deeds:

your lessons of what
            may never
                  stay,

how
   atmospheres emerge,
                  disperse,

or why precipitations build

(and, when they leave,
why they return)

or what must reel
               on its way,

or how sun cures obscurity

−and then

      the windowed universe
      you selflessly unveil for us,
      so we should glimpse
      beyond ourselves,
      our times,
      the trappings of our world.

I've often
been the onlooker,
absorbing your abstracted scenes,
vague lines behind your muted hues
contrasting with your passing signs,
your ever-changing artistry
of momentary sculptures,
drafts,
the dramas of your shadow plays,
or spectral canvases
you've stretched
throughout my
mental galleries.

Then I turn artist,
teasing shapes,

the poet scoping likenesses
in any given cumulus:

an open hand,
a horse,
a heart,
a lion,
dragon,

flame,

a face.

At times,
   I'll be the seeker, too,
      observing moons,
the noontime sun,
their rays that reach
      right round an edge
like searchlights
   probing
      unknown
         gaps.

My wondering
   runs
      much
         like that:

faint fingers falling
            into fog
until they brush
solidity,

or spaces where they'll
      pull back drapes,
            reveal
         long-concealed
   truths.

You foster curiosity,
more sprightly minds,
            inventiveness,
refashioning,
kinetic
      and adaptive views,

      the fluctuation of what is,
the manifestation of all change,
      the newness that shall ever be,
            the vital ebbs,
                        activity,
            resuscitation,
      renaissance,
mythology
 as I divine
      clandestine whales
            from cirrus wisps,
               as if I'm Ahab
         chasing fate.

   You've moved me to
               philosophy,
                  to contemplate
                  the world
                  of forms,
                  perfected
                  things
            above the

clouds,
removed
from flaws
and
imitations
of our

most
imperfect
sphere.

My questioning
ascends on high
like birds, or geese,
            or eagles way
above your most
            secluded clouds.

I've soared in thoughts
    above your storms,
your rain clouds
        of ten trillion tears,
    your thunderheads
about to burst,
        your hurricanes
            and lightning strikes
            and I have been
        electrified.

I've drowned
in your enormity,
been awed by your
raw forcefulness,
how you envelop
everything,
beginning with
this level earth
that's yawning
toward eternity.

Your wind's
the wind
which lets me breathe

then takes my breath
and blends my breath
with many other exhalations:

smokestacks,
songs from other lungs,
discharge of cars,
the gas of swamps,
organic things,
the pollen,
the volcano's belch,
the breath of forests,
mist of seas,
the oxygen

the living
breathe.

Though overcast,
  you've made it clear:

there is no Earth
  as we know Earth,

no life
like now,

no blue
on high,

no
heavens
dreamt

without you,
sky.

Entwined

Offline, outdoors, nearby, away,
a billion threads invisibly
entwine us, bind you, link me to
all moments, persons, places, things
before, behind, well out of mind.

At no time are we severed, lost, detached
from who or how or why I was,
or where you stand, by land or sea.
As far we try to cut and run,
the world's wide net entangles us.

But we're no helpless catches now:
we'll glide like spiders through the silk,
traverse the swerving strands with ease,
because what ties us frees us, too,
from notions of irrelevance.

Relationships, ecology,
environments of earth—to be:
fine fibers of our vital web
unite us tight, much closer here,
and this is nothing one should fear.

The Daring of the Roadside Deer

Another luckless deer along the highway's lines,
as if it fell asleep beneath the rusting rail
and won't wake up.

It kills me every time I spot a loss like that.

And it should hit us, yes.

We ought to register pain,
be willing to envision that experience:

the sunlit pasture after dandelion hills,
a yawning morning's grazing,
fearless frolicking,

two young deer strolling slowly into sunlit woods,
maneuvering around low limbs
and squeezing past
the crunchy clumps of brush
and messy beds of mottled leaves,

the slightly older deer about to cross the road,
as is its right.

Imagine the clash,
those tender seconds
just before:

four tawny legs to press ahead
of mid-March grass,
enduring the obstinate dark
of asphalt lanes

—and then the horn,

the rubber screeching,

lethal glare,

then every green scene,

gold and red sights

night at once

—so suddenly, some wonder
was there agony?

The deer's unblinking eyes
dare we stare back,

share in its crash,

sense deprivation,

empathize,

or recognize
how much we've died.

Repose

I'm back from work.
Four deer nap near
the backyard oak.

I step soft, walk
so slowly past
the noisy gate.

When they're not here,
I'll open it
and let it sing,

but not today:
they need their peace,
these quiet times.

They've had too much
of stunning noise,
life on the run.

I go home through
another door,
relieved they sleep.

Their restfulness
becomes my peace,
my conscience eased.

Earthward

I turn toward Earth, escaping space,
that coldest place of comforting,
which gives you distance, solitude,
an endless sea of stars to rove,
yet nothing that approaches home,
the weight and firmness of a world
where one could stand or fall and land
instead of drifting aimlessly
into a deathless emptiness.

Our rockets promised reveries,
inflaming dreams of other orbs
where we would scheme new genesis,
creations made to serve our ways,
remaking planets as we want,
according to our claims and needs,
because we let ourselves believe
the universe belongs to us
and humans might succeed as gods.

No, we are fleshly, mortal things,
imperfect and ephemeral
—at most forever part of this
atomic cosmic medium,
where energies endure all time—
but no one should elude this truth:
there is no other residence,
no habitat except this dirt,
this mud and dust, these clumps of clay.

So I return to Earth today
to kiss the gritty ground again,
abound in daylight, gravity,
rejoice in rocks, impermanence,
the finite rivers, grains of sand,
because I've come to understand
evasion's what we leave behind
when we dwell in reality.
Then life is ours. Then we're free.

Versed in Earth

Don't search for Earth
inside these lines,

or hope to find
completed trees,

the qualities
of one lone stone,

or partial fine print
of a leaf.

No real river
bends through here:

one water drop
speaks volumes more.

Please roam outdoors.
Bear witness. Learn.

Approach the forests.
Hear their tales.

Consult the boulders,
Birds and dirt.

Go ask the canyons
how to sing.

Attend the concerts
of the wheat,

the mountain's poems
to the sky,

the eloquence of wind
and rain,

the epics of each ant
and plant,

for they will teach you
what I can't.

Fields of Study

I've turned to nature, searching for new truths,
fresh strategies, instructions, clarity
—some indication now my soul runs right
or that I'm nearing where I ought to be,
approaching progress, on an honest path
that places beings closer to the start
—square one, renewal, human renaissance—
or purposes and lots to be revealed,
appreciated, understood, fulfilled.

The function of a stream, the aim of bees,
the motives of the polar bear or mole,
objectives of the cheetah, bison, hawk,
intentions of the mouse, the skunk, or elk,
or impulses of horses, goats, or wolves
all differ as to creed or need or speed,
and yet I find much kinship, overlap
between their aspirations and my world,
and so I study them like earth itself.

As for their answers to my questions, well,
I'm learning still, I have to say, each day,
examining the rabbit's patterns, geese
and crows and hummingbirds and how they go
about their business, like the cow, the cat,
the antelope of curving horns, the dogs
all barking at the furtive fox, the deer,
who never seek to bother anyone,
like the koala, panda, and the sloth.

Each plant responds to me in its own way:
the clover and the wild thyme say grow,
as does the moss along abiding pines,
which tell me I may stay and yet ascend.
Then limestone preaches steadiness and strength,
while light and water teach me to sustain,
be energy, exist to help the rest.
I'm still their student in this course of life,
preparing for its lessons, every test.

Reckoning

How many suns
  impassion us?

How many moons
  enrapture us?

How many stars
  rekindle us?

How many dreams
  awaken us?

And how many hours
  count our love?

The honest answer is
  too few.

Little Gratitudes

I thank you, heartbeats,
sunrise, breath,

each easy breeze
that's parting drapes,

the rains which didn't
rain too long,

you, leaning fence,
who holds the line,

returning birdsong,
grass of spring,

these evergreen,
perennials,

another noon
to laud the small.

Going Speechless

I should be dumbstruck at this crag,
impressed by trees five times my age,
surprised by boulders thrice my height

—but no,

I'm jotting concepts down,

>describing,
>rhyming,
>dreaming,
>scheming complicated metaphors,

because I've done this
since my youth.

You'd think, by now, I'd plainly see
the irony of noting things
which only thrive here
—in this land—
beyond the burdens of my words.

For instance, take that waterfall:

>its energies so generous,
>its forceful flows
>—although its ease,

the way it shimmers,
skips,
then gives its wealth
so freely to our world

"like diamonds poured by bucketloads"?

—there's poverty in loftiness,
extravagance's vanity,
obsession with embellishments,

and I have often wrongly guessed
I might describe the generous sky,
large charities of precious light,
the altruism of this earth,

instead of me just witnessing,

just standing there and witnessing,

what must be free of utterance,
relieved of our most perfect verbs,
our nonpareil adjectives.

Such gracious nature needs no further verse
because it lives and breathes the primal poetry
born of the earth, the cosmic flame,
the Poem Prime preceding time.

Such grandeur calls for selflessness,

the meekness of a mindfulness
reflecting deep respectfulness.

I offer up my speechlessness.

Before, Ahead

We're sweeping leaves we swept before
because we didn't bag them up.

Now wind plays mischief, hide and seek,
and leaps into dead foliage.

But that's okay: this lets us talk,
my wife and I. We reminisce.

This was her grandpa's yard before.
He set those stone stairs in this hill.

Back then, they hung clothes on the line,
and trains came by and shook the panes.

I hold her while she recollects.
I love her love of history,

her hopes and goals, her life before
she hugged me when I knelt, proposed.

And we discuss the future, too:
the home and roads ahead of us.

Sometime we'll walk, let all this go,
just like the forest: sweet release.

New owners come. We'll move ahead,
seed gardens in another yard,

scale other hills, embrace the gray,
and welcome winds which visit us

as we recline and golden leaves
weave blankets for these memories.

Succession

Unnumbered soles
wore down stone stairs
for centuries up grassy slopes.

Now mushrooms, moss,
with clumps of phlox
ascend instead, reclaim these ways,

erase the trace
of human passage,
repossessing step by step,

by blade and leaf,
each clustered bloom,
deposing what was once imposed,

recycling earth,
returning rocks
back underground where new life forms,

emergent
and eventually
suggesting structure, order, paths,

conveyance
and continuance,
until the next succession
comes.

Afterwords

Essay: On the Vitality of Nature Poems

I believe in the vitality, relevance, and significance of nature poetry. It's why I've devoted so many efforts to exploring and expressing earthly and environmental themes since I aspired to be a poet decades ago. For me, writing about nature is not only a delightful and intriguing pursuit; it's an entirely essential and beneficial endeavor driven primarily by a human need to connect, to contemplate, and a natural inclination to celebrate and preserve the world for future generations.

I find I *must* observe nature, must regard creation with humility, reverence, and patience, and I should meditate upon it at length, trying my personal best to comprehend some part of it before I discuss it or share any thoughts about it through my poetry. Through that necessary mindfulness, I might gain some insights and comprehend life a little bit more, which then would allow me to participate more consciously, creatively, and positively in this existence we share with other humans, living things, and the planet.

Despite my passion for the subject, I realize there is an opposite perspective to consider: not everyone sees nature poems the way I do. Not everyone shares in that passion or would elevate subjects such as earth or life to the extent I do. As a result, nature poems don't always receive the readership or respect I believe they could or should. It also means being a "nature poet" can be something of a challenge when readers anticipate something more visibly personal and centered upon expressly human emotions.

From my conversations with readers and poets over the years, I understand some people much prefer the rawness, immediacy, vulnerability, and shock value of what some people have described as "confessional poetry," which focuses on individual situations and experiences, inner thoughts, and responses to a wide range of topics, such as love, solitude, regrets, desires, memories, and more. Many readers see those poems as being more relatable, intense, perceptive, and revealing than nature poems.

Poetry, like all forms of expression, is subject to subjective thoughts, personal insights and emotions, among other things, and this is one of the strengths and most inclusive aspects of written and artistic expression: artists, readers, observers, and critics can all regard the same creation and maintain diverse views, interpretations, and reactions. This is how literature, poetry, and all forms of art can mean so many things to many different people at different times in history.

We humans feel and reply to the external world. We each have specific expectations, experiences, preferences based on those happenings, individual aesthetics, intelligence, and feelings, and these things influence our judgement of literary and artistic works. As for myself, as a poet who began as a child who loved poetry, I'm of the opinion that, when compared against the best confessional verse, many of the best nature poems can exhibit comparable qualities which can affect readers profoundly and personally, all while relating individual impressions, desires, questions, and experiences with the self, other living things, the environment, and the larger world.

Appreciable intimacies can be found and felt in many nature poems, especially when those poems include specific and vivid imagery which can help ground the words in an organic reality we may envision, recognize, be surprised by, or react to substantially as individuals. The best nature poets can move us just as well as any other kind of poet, as they also have the power to confide, to startle, to endear or bare, and to offer up heartfelt and revelatory verses we may consider stirring, candid, alluring, sensuous, abstract or concrete, philosophical, spiritual, human, unguarded, conflicted, delicate, delightful, furious, traumatic, lyrical, or uniquely impassioned.

It is the nature poem that can bring images and aspects from the external world into the private chambers of our minds, the secret sanctum of consciousness and sensitivities, and it is the nature poem that allows us to experience something that includes the self yet can transcend the self to embrace the larger context of life, Earth, the environment, and ultimately the universe and the collective magnificence of creation.

Observations and truths emerging from these poetic nature experiences can be just as urgent, fiery, soulful, poignant, and powerful as confessional poems in their impacts on readers. Nature poems can romanticize, haunt, manifest heartbreak, or hearten us with their words, which can whisper, coo, howl, sigh, groan or moan, fear or cheer, grieve, relieve, lament, repent, or blaze with sublime light or ecstatic torrents of emotional epiphanies. In other words, nature poems can be confessional, too.

And nature poems can go even further, becoming potential tools for personal introspection and interpersonal insights. They can stun us and educate us as much as they might entertain us or philosophize about life and love, and they can be part of our personal and societal searches for more organic and objective truths, more creative comparisons and connections, and they may even contribute to community or spiritual development, to scientific understanding, and many other aspects of our lives.

Beyond that, I strongly believe some nature poems have the potential to redeem and preserve—and that they may save us, in some manner, by helping us to treasure Earth and spare our world from dangerous and undesirable futures. As ideological, economical, technological, and environmental challenges continue to endanger the well-being of Earth and its inhabitants, it is the nature poem that can remind us of the life outside of our walls. It is the nature poem that can help us remember or restore our humanity as we turn from the artificial and the selfish to rediscover, share, and embrace the more natural and open world.

That appears to be an ambitious claim, but I would encourage you to think about it: any poem that has the potential of moving someone to regard and respect nature more positively and intimately is a poem that helps to save humanity and the world. When enough people care sufficiently for life and the environment, there may be preservation, continuance of life, a thriving that's preserved for coming generations. When the opposite happens, and we have fewer people who appreciate nature, Earth stands to suffer, as does humanity. Who could possibly want that?

But that's not the end of the matter: as it turns out, I have found nature poems can do and mean many things. Here are some examples drawn from my own experiences as a reader of poetry and as a poet:

Nature poems could...
- ...help us to rediscover and explore ourselves and our beautiful planet
- ...enable us to make more personal and shared connections with the natural world
- ...encourage us to learn about habitats, organic processes, and living things

- …let us learn and eventually care about natural things, counteracting human issues such as desensitization, disconnectedness, and apathy
- …preserve regional environmental history and related observations
- …educate us on various environmental issues and considerations
- …inspire us to consider human nature and what it means to be alive
- …compel us to celebrate and nurture living things
- …convince us to conserve natural resources and use them more mindfully
- …provoke us to pursue sustainable practices and materials
- …unify us as earthlings with mutual interests in survival and a healthy world
- …remind us that we human are part of nature, planet Earth, and the universe
- …prompt us to mind and resolve environmentally dangerous phenomena
- …urge us to evaluate and improve upon our influences over nature
- …nurture our empathy and strengthen our community bonds

This isn't what I'd consider an exhaustive list, but I hope at least one of those points begin to show how nature poems deserve more serious consideration and respect.

Another wish of mine is that you will have more opportunities to encounter other poets—far better poets—who have written substantially about the natural world—poets such as Basho, John Clare, Walt Whitman, Robert Frost, Gary Snyder, Wendell Berry, Mary Oliver, and Joy Harjo, among others.

In addition to those works, there are a number of nature poem anthologies you might enjoy. A librarian at your nearest public library can help you find one or more of these books. Eventually, you might also consider writing some nature poetry of your own, if you haven't done so already.

Reading and writing poetry, especially nature poetry, continues to help me to observe and contemplate the world more meaningfully, and to exist and explore life more completely, and to appreciate Earth's generosity more deeply, such that I can feel and express my gratitude toward nature more fully and sincerely. The positivity and insights emerging from these realizations can be so beautiful and moving, so profoundly purposeful and life-affirming, so exhilarating and enlightening, that I would really love for you and many others to enjoy and prosper from these kinds of naturally wonderful experiences as well!

About the Author

Robert J. Tiess is a poet, nature lover, musician, and artist living in New York State all his life. A SUNY New Paltz University graduate with a degree in English Literature, Robert has been writing poetry since the 1980s. Since the 1990s he has pursued a joyful career in public library service. In September 2022, Robert married the love of his life, Sandra.

For even more about the poet, please see the autobiographical portions of his debut poetry collection, ***The Humbling and Other Poems***.

You can also visit Robert's website at
www.RobertJTiess.net

197

Other Books by the Author

Available in print and electronic formats.

The Humbling and Other Poems

This inspiring and critically-acclaimed debut poetry collection features over 100 accessible and imaginative poems on relatable themes such as hope, love, justice, peace, humility, and more. There is "something for everyone" to be found in this memorable poetic journey.

As part of Robert's ongoing efforts to promote accessibility and public participation in poetry, he has included a glossary of poetry terms, poetry reading suggestions, three brief essays, as well as some autobiographical writing, and more in this book.

May We Learn from the Earth: Nature Poems and Reflections on the Environment

Clear, captivating, and compassionate poetry contemplating Earth and nature.

From the opening poems, we become reacquainted with the natural realm, where we may muse on mountains, reflect on rivers, philosophize in forests, and celebrate creation everywhere.

As we journey into Earth, the Beautiful, studying its rivers, canyons, trees, and fields, we learn and grow more mindful of the environment, ecology, and eventually Earth, the Besieged.

Insightful, inspiring, and impassioned with a lyrical love of life, this timely and truthful collection can be enjoyed by nearly everyone, from budding poetry enthusiasts and nature lovers to environmental champions and beyond.

In hopes of encouraging environmental interest and awareness, the author offers optional reading content, including a series of brief but thought-provoking essays meditating on nature, a concise glossary of Earth terms, reading suggestions, and more for readers to discover and explore.